# *Write Your Way to a Successful Scholarship Essay*

CANDACE CHAMBERS

Copyright © 2018 Candace Chambers

All rights reserved.

ISBN-13: 978-1981455478
ISBN-10: 1981455477

# DEDICATION

This guide is dedicated to Dr. Jean Chamberlain, who encouraged me to soar, and challenged me to help other students achieve their full potential.

## CONTENTS

Preface i
Introduction iii

1. Searching for Scholarships — 1
2. Understanding the Prompt — Pg 8
3. Writing the Introduction — Pg 13
4. Writing the Body Paragraphs — Pg 18
5. Setting Yourself Apart — Pg 23
6. Writing the Conclusion — Pg 30
7. Revising and Editing — Pg 31
8. Saving/Recycling the Essay — Pg 38
9. Practice Writing the Essay — Pg 39
10. Uses of Scholarship Funds — Pg 44

Conclusion — Pg 47

Sample Winning Scholarship Essay — Pg 48

Resources — Pg 53

About the Author — Pg 56

# PREFACE

As a high school senior, I searched for scholarships daily. I knew that scholarships were going to be my sources of funds for college. Moving forward, when I was an undergraduate student, I had to learn about the rules of money at a fast pace. Since I transferred schools after my first semester of college, I did not qualify for freshman scholarships because I was not a first-time freshman. So, I had to rely on federal financial aid and outside scholarships to fund my academic endeavors.

It was during my freshman year of college that I realized that I must learn how to continuously apply for scholarships. I learned to budget and save the scholarship money I received as this skill would be crucial to my experience in college.

And I did. I graduated from undergrad with no student loans, a fruitful college experience, and $20,000 in savings.

But, what was my technique? How did I learn? It was not rocket science. Just commitment.

Since I had to fund my education 100%, I applied for many scholarships throughout my academic journey. I was awarded national, state, and local scholarships.

One thing I learned was that many students stray away from scholarships that involve the writing of an essay. The reason is because essays scare people. The task of sitting down and writing thoughts in a constructive way is intimidating for some. Due to this observation, I discovered that competition was lower for scholarship competitions that required essays.

Some scholarships I was awarded were the Regions Riding Forward Scholarship ($2,500), Thurgood Marshall College Fund: Costco Scholarship ($6,200), and the Conference on College, Composition, and Communication- Scholar for the Dream Travel Award ($1,000).

It is my hope that sharing my story will help other students learn the value of a scholarship essay!

- Candace Chambers

# INTRODUCTION

College can be an exciting time for many students as they navigate through academic courses and gain life-changing experiences. Often times, fruitful college experiences are a result of the financial security to afford college expenses. Many parents fund the financial costs of their students, and may have also saved money for their children to attend college. On the contrary, some students have the task of securing funds each semester of their collegiate tenure.

As the costs of tuition, fees, supplies, and books rise, many parents and students must supplement funds and fill in the gaps of uncovered financial costs. The Bureau of Labor Statistics reports the following: "From January 2006 to July 2016, the Consumer Price Index for college tuition and fees increased 63 percent, compared with an increase of 21 percent for all items. Over that period, consumer prices for college textbooks increased 88 percent and housing at school increased 51 percent," (Bureau of Labor Statistics).

Scholarships are often the go-to sources of monies to help students become financially secure during college. High school seniors as well as college students search for scholarships to help them pay for expenses. Many scholarships require the writing of an essay to be eligible for funds, and this requirement often deters students from composing the essay. Therefore, this guide will provide students with steps to composing a scholarship essay that can enable students to enjoy college with less worry about financial costs!

***Disclaimer:** This guide does not guarantee the winning of a scholarship essay. This guide only provides tips and steps for writers to compose the scholarship essay.

# 1. SEARCHING FOR SCHOLARSHIPS

Before writing a scholarship essay, begin researching the various types of scholarships that are available in multiple arenas. The word, "research," can be intimidating for some, but performing a Google search is a form of research. Whether you are trying to determine when the latest phone will be released or the most recent football scores, you are attempting to find more information about a particular topic, therefore researching.

When locating scholarships, you will need to dedicate time to thoroughly search through various websites. Initial research terms in your favorite search engine (Google, Bing, etc.), can be, "scholarships for high school students," or "scholarships for college students." Although the terms are general, they can begin your search and lead to more specific scholarships. Also, these search terms may lead to websites that contain lists of available scholarships for students who are athletes, reside in different states, of various cultural or ethnic backgrounds, or who excel academically.

Other results may lead to scholarships offered by national companies, states, local clubs or organizations, or colleges and universities. An explanation of each is below:

**National Scholarships:** Companies such as Nissan USA, Burger King, and Coca-Cola offer scholarships to students nationwide based on different criteria. Some of these companies target specific demographics of students, while others offer the scholarship funds to any student who applies. Applying for national scholarships allows you to compete with students on a national level, and if awarded the scholarship, the recognition is often broadcasted nationwide. But, I will advise you not to place all of your focus on searching and applying only for national scholarships due to the greater pool of applicants. Applying for 1-3 national scholarships can provide you with a chance to win without placing all hope into one category of scholarships.

A list of some national scholarships retrieved from a 2018 search are as follows:

1. GE-Reagan Foundation Scholarship Program- up to $40,000 per recipient
2. Gates Millennium Scholars- "Funding for the full cost of attendance* that is not already covered by other financial aid and the expected family contribution, as determined by the Free Application for Federal Student Aid."

3. Ron Brown Scholar Program- $40,000
4. Foot Locker Scholar Athletes- $20,000
5. Regions Riding Forward Scholarship Essay Contest- $5,000 (High School Students) and $3,000 (College Students)

**State Scholarships**: States often set aside funds to support their student residents with scholarships and grants. These funds may stem from the state's educational fund or even from the state's lottery. According to the National Association of Student Financial Aid Administrators (NASFAA), "almost every state education agency has at least one grant or scholarship available to residents, and many have a long list of student aid programs." Sometimes students must attend a college within their state of residence in order to qualify for state financial aid. These sources of aid may want students to provide the financial status of their parents or guardians which can be retrieved through the Free Application for Federal Student Aid (FAFSA). The FAFSA, offered through the U.S. Department of Education is "responsible for managing the student financial assistance programs authorized under Title IV of the Higher Education Act of 1965. These programs provide grants, loans, and work-study funds to students attending college or career school. should be completed by all students." It is advised that all students complete the FAFSA, no matter the income level of their parents or guardians.

I advise all students who plan to attend or are currently attending school in-state to apply for state aid throughout their collegiate journey. Visit the NASFAA's website to locate financial aid in your state.

Examples of state aid sources are below:
- New York- New York State Tuition Assistance Program (TAP)
- Arizona- Arizona Commission for Postsecondary Education (ACPE)
- Tennessee- Education Lottery Programs
- California- California Student Aid Commission
- Michigan- Michigan Student Aid

**Local Scholarships:** Various clubs and organizations within communities offer scholarships for local residents in order to provide financial support for those who live and contribute to the community. Often times, these local organizations will send their scholarship offers directly to local school counselors, whether high school or college. These scholarships are sometimes less than $1,000, but obtaining multiple small scholarships can add up! In addition, many employers offer scholarships to their employees or dependents of their employees. Therefore, ask your counselor, your parent, or your employer (if you are working) all throughout the year about scholarships.

Examples of Local Scholarships:

- Walmart Foundation Associate Scholarship
- University of Mississippi Medical Center: Child of Faculty Award/Staff Award
- Humana Foundation Scholarships

- Wells Fargo Team Members Dependent Scholarship Program
- Sorority and Fraternity Scholarships
- Rotary Foundations

**Institutional Scholarships**: Incoming and current college students have opportunities to apply for scholarships through institutions of higher learning. These scholarships are offered through merit-based criteria, athletics, community service efforts, leadership roles, and musical talents, to name a few. Also, some alumni and community members contribute funds for endowment, legacy, or development scholarships, which are usually housed separately from merit scholarships at institutions for qualifying students. Contact your financial aid department and ask for the available scholarships for incoming or current students. You may have to complete one financial aid application to apply for all institutional scholarships, but some scholarships may have to be applied for individually.

I advise students to apply for institutional scholarships because they can often obtain the funds by meeting the criteria and without having to compete against other applicants.

Examples of Institutional Scholarships:

- Phi Beta Kappa Scholarships
- Veteran Scholarships
- Transfer Scholarships (Community College Students)
- ACT/SAT Scholarships

- Valedictorian/Salutatorian Scholarships
- Luckyday Success Scholarships
- Star Athlete Scholarships
- High Achieving GPA Scholarships
- National Merit Scholarship Program

The search for scholarships can be tedious, but taking the time to find those potential sources of money will be well worth the time!

# Your Turn to Write!

Perform a Google Search. Write down some of the scholarships you qualify for and would like to apply!

| SCHOLARSHIP | DEADLINE |
|---|---|
| | |
| | |
| | |
| | |
| | |
| | |
| | |

## 2. UNDERSTANDING THE PROMPT

Many scholarship offers ask a question or provide a statement for the applicant to respond. This inquiry is often called a prompt. The prompt may be one sentence, two sentences, or even a paragraph. It is your job to dissect the prompt, so you can understand your task of writing the scholarship essay.

Examples of essay prompts include:

- How will the funds assist you in furthering your education?

- What are your career goals?

- How can you impact your community after graduation?

- Who is someone that has made an influence in your life? Why?

Let's dissect the following prompt from the 2018 Regions Riding Forward Scholarship Essay Contest:

"Who inspires you? Is there a particular African-American who inspires you because of the significant achievements in our society that he or she has been responsible for? In 500 words or less: Address how an African-American has been an inspiration in your life. Discuss the contributions of the African-American individual who has served to inspire and motivate you."

By taking an initial look at the prompt, we can identify keywords that are repeated and are significant to the meaning of the prompt.

Using the prompt above, keywords may include:

- inspires/inspiration
- African American
- achievements
- motivation
- you

You will also need to make a note of the word count or page limit of the response. For this prompt, the word count for the essay is 500 words or less.

Now that you have identified keywords from the prompt and the word count, begin brainstorming ways that you plan to address the question or statement. You may have different ideas and directions that you want to pursue in response to the prompt, which is okay! The more ideas you have, the more options you will have in answering the prompt. Just in case one idea does not blossom as you planned, you can have other ones to refer to.

For the 2018 Regions Riding Forward Scholarship Essay Contest, some ideas to discuss may include:

- An African American mother/father who has achieved many accomplishments and has inspired you to attend college as a first-generation college student
- An African American mentor, teacher, community member who dedicates his time to be sure that you succeed as a student
- An African American civil rights leader or public figure in the past or the present who fought/fights for issues of racial inequality and inspires you to fight for justice in your future career as a defense lawyer

All of these ideas address the requirements from the prompt, and therefore are suitable starting points for the scholarship essay. Draft ideas in a location that can save your work, so you can refer to them while writing your scholarship essay.

As you continue to focus your topic, continuously create brainstorming sessions in environments which cultivate your inner creativity. Sometimes it is helpful for writers to create an atmosphere conducive to concentration such as a library or a quiet room. Others concentrate better with music or background television noise. Whatever environment is best for you, create that space. Sometimes you may want to brainstorm on the go. Ideas may come as you walk around campus, in the grocery store, or even in a dream! Write down those ideas or type them in the notes section of a device, so you can keep them in a central location.

Also, while brainstorming, it is helpful to stay organized. I advise creating an outline of your thoughts once you finish brainstorming. Additionally, use organizational tools such as bubble maps and Venn diagrams to structure your thoughts. Bubble Maps help to organize ideas in a circle-based format. Venn diagrams show relationships between concepts. For example, a bubble map will be a useful tool if you had to provide reasons why you needed scholarship funds in school. In the circles, you could write supplies, meal plan, books, and tuition. A Venn diagram can be used if you had to compare/contrast your past self to your present self while discussing your growth over the years. The diagram will provide a visual of your ideas in order to help you organize your thoughts to respond to the prompt. Drafting these organizational maps on a dry-erase board or post-it notes can also provide visual representations of your thoughts as you work to organize them effectively.

# Your Turn to Write!

Dissect the prompt below. Identify the keywords. Then, make a list of ideas that relate to the prompt.

"What are your goals? How can college help you achieve your goals? If awarded the scholarship funds, how do you plan to use them?"

Keywords:

- _____
- _____
- _____
- _____
- _____

Ideas:

_____

_____

_____

_____

_____

## 3. WRITING THE INTRODUCTION

At this step, you will now begin writing the scholarship essay. Writing is a process that takes time and much focus. Therefore, allow yourself time to compose your scholarship essay. Many times, thoughts and ideas will come over the course of days or weeks, so you want to dedicate the time for content development. The dedication of time helps you to be able to plan your essay more efficiently.

As you prepare to write the introduction to your scholarship essay, think of a way to bring the reader into your writing in a creative way. Some ways may include as follows:

**Anecdote:** Tell a short story that is interesting and preferably explains an occurrence that happened to you.

*Example*: "My third grade teacher introduced me to Ms. Claudette Colvin. She read a short story about the 15 year old girl who refused to give up her seat on the bus in Montgomery, Alabama. That day, Ms. Colvin became my hero."

**Quotation:** Locate a quote from someone that connects to your topic of discussion.

*Example:* "Success isn't about how much money you make, it's about the difference you make in people's lives."- Michelle Obama

**Definition:** Define a key term that is central to your essay. Always include the name of the source where you obtained the definition.

*Example:* "Hero is defined by Merriam Webster dictionary as 'a person admired for achievements and noble qualities, and one who shows great courage.'"

**Facts/ Statistics:** Research various facts or statistics that relate to your essay. Remember to include the source of the findings.

*Example:* "According to the Center for Disease Control and Prevention, 'A poor diet can lead to energy imbalance (e.g., eating more calories than your body uses) and can increase the risk of becoming overweight or obese.'"

**Create a Scene:** Describe a scene vividly using all 5 senses and take the reader on a journey to that place.

*Example:* "As I walked down the hall passing nursing stations on my left and my right, I anxiously approached Room 818C. The sound of monitoring machines rang loudly as I walked in. Little did I know that these final seconds would be the last time I saw breath move through my mother's body."

These various ways to approach the introduction of your scholarship essay can allow for an interesting read for your reader. Experiment with various approaches for your introduction and choose the one that provides the most details and is the most relevant to the subject of your essay.

Once you have determined the approach you would like to use, begin writing the essay. The first 2-3 sentences can be general information about the topic using one of the approaches above. Then proceed with becoming more specific to your topic with the next 2-3 sentences. The last 2 sentences should state your topic as specific as possible. These last sentences will also include your thesis statement.

A **thesis statement** is the sum total of your essay in a sentence or sometimes two. This statement should be as clear and concise as possible.

*Example:* "Since college costs are expensive, I would use the funds to supplement the cost of tuition and fees if awarded the scholarship.

This thesis statement explains how the writer will use the funds in a direct, concise, sentence, so the reader knows the answer to the t before reading the entire essay. Sometimes it takes more time to compose a thesis statement than writing the body paragraphs. My advice is to draft a preliminary thesis statement before writing the body paragraphs. If you have to revise the thesis statement after writing the body paragraphs, then go back to your statement and align the ideas from the essay.

# Your Turn to Write!

If you had to introduce yourself to a stranger, what would you write about yourself? In one paragraph, describe yourself in a creative way, but be clear as possible.

## 4. WRITING THE BODY PARAGRAPHS

When writing your scholarship essay, the body paragraphs provide extensive detail of your response. These paragraphs are the meat of the essay. I suggest writers compose three body paragraphs for their scholarship essay, so they will have enough information for the reader to grasp an understanding of their response to the topic.

The body paragraphs should be in logical order, but sometimes it is helpful to write all of your thoughts down first, then go back and organize them logically.

*Example:*

**Body Paragraph 1:** Learning the game of football
**Body Paragraph 2:** Winning Athletic Awards
**Body Paragraph 3:** Compare being a champion in the game of football to a champion in life

In your body paragraphs, refer back to the prompt often to ensure that you are addressing every aspect of the prompt. Other pointers to address when composing your body paragraphs are explained by topic below:

## Transitions

Transitions assist with guiding your reader from one thought to the next. They also can show relationship between ideas and the significance of ideas. Transitions are bolded in the examples below.

*Example 1:*

- "**To begin,** I am the first child in my family to go to college. My parents are unable to help me navigate college, but I have decided to pursue higher education. **Therefore,** I need financial, academic, and professional support."

*Example 2:*

- "**Second,** I plan to use the knowledge I have gained in my degree program to provide social services to children. **Specifically,** I plan to help children who are disadvantaged and in need of food and shelter."

As shown in these examples, the transitions move the reader from one topic to the next and also inform the reader of the relationship between thoughts. In the first example, "to begin" implies that the statement was the reader's first point like "second" implies that the statement was the reader's second point. "Specifically" and "therefore" add support to the statements as well as draw direct attention to the points brought forth. Overall, transitions serve as links between ideas to guide the reader from one point to the next. A list of more transitions is included in the "Resources" section of the guide.

**Topic Sentences**

Topic sentences begin each paragraph as they explain the main idea that is to follow. It is vital to have a topic sentence for each of your body paragraphs because they guide the reader through your claims in your essay. Without a topic sentence, the reader may be unsure of your plan of action in your paragraph. Stray away from beginning your topic sentences with, "In this paper, I am going to tell you…" or "In the next sentence, I am going to explain…" An example of a topic sentence is as follows:

"I have always dreamed of going to college because I want to participate in internships that can help me reach my goal of becoming a civil engineer."

The topic sentence explains the intentions of the writer as he or she begins her paragraph. The writer's plan for the paragraph may be to explain different ways he or she can obtain internships, the benefits of internships, and how he or she can use the experiences to reach their career goals.

## Point of View

When composing your scholarship essay, I would advise writing in the first-person point of view. This point of view can establish a connection with the reader as you explain your personal viewpoints and reasons for wanting the scholarship. First person point of view includes pronouns such as "I," "me," and "my." Try to avoid using second person or third person point of view since you want to be as direct as possible for your reader.

Finally, always be aware of the word count while writing your body paragraphs to avoid disqualification. My advice would be to write as much as possible, then delete unnecessary portions of the essay, which we will discuss in the Revising and Editing chapter.

# Your Turn to Write!

How would you organize events in your life that involve your journey in school? Did you win an important award in elementary school? Were you the star basketball player in middle school? Did you achieve 1st chair in the band as a senior? Jot down a few events in order below.

| Event | Significance |
|---|---|
| 1. | |
| 2. | |
| 3. | |
| 4. | |

## 5. SETTING YOURSELF APART

Scholarship essay committees often read multiple essays at a time and sometimes in one setting. I can imagine that reading the same type of essay, which may lack creativity or variety, can become mundane for the readers. Similarly structured essays could be placed in one lumped pile of essays because they do not catch the attention of the reader. Since a variety of readers may be reading your essay, your job is to set yourself apart from other applicants.

One way you can set yourself apart is by sharing some of your favorite experiences. The readers of your scholarship essay are eager to hear your voice and learn about your life. So, share information that is personal to you that you believe others would enjoy learning about. Allow yourself the time to develop your ideas by adding details, including the most important information, and creating an interesting read for your readers that can be memorable.

You can also set yourself apart by effectively utilizing three rhetorical appeals: logos, ethos, and pathos.

- Logos is the use of logical appeal. Your job is to try to persuade the reader to believe your claim or argument using facts, statistics, or other types of proof to support your claim. These forms of evidence should come from reputable sources such as peer-reviewed journals, books, and websites ending in .gov, .edu, .mil, and .com if the organization or source is credible. You can also use cause and effect to explain your claims. Your job is to persuade the scholarship essay reader using logic that your essay deserves to be the awarded submission.

  - **Example of Logos:** "My community needs services for elderly residents because many of them do have the necessary medical services to assist them if they fall. The Center for Disease and Control and Prevention reports, "Health care providers can play an important role in fall prevention by 1) screening older adults for fall risk, 2) reviewing and managing medications linked to falls, and 3) recommending vitamin D where appropriate for improved bone, muscle, and nerve health." Therefore, I want to become a healthcare provider in my community because elderly patients are at risk.

    - **Explanation:** The excerpt above employs the logical appeal of logos by connecting Point A (the community is in the need of assistance for elderly residents if they encounter a fall) to Point B (healthcare providers can play an important role in assisting elderly citizens) to Point C (I want to be a healthcare provider in my community). The writer also uses a statistic from a reputable source: the Center for Disease Control and Prevention.

- Ethos is the use of the ethical appeal. Your credibility as a writer is the foundation for the ethical appeal. Since you are the expert of your writing, you automatically have the power to convince your reader that you are worthy of the scholarship award. You want to write your essay so your reader can trust that you are the expert in the subject. Ways you can establish ethos include showing your expertise in a subject and by providing evidence to your claims.

    o **Example of Ethos:** "I have been a musician since the age of 5. My mother enrolled me in beginner piano courses when I expressed that I wanted to become a famous piano player. Throughout my years of playing the piano, I have explored the worlds of Beethoven, Bach, and Scott Joplin. My experiences of playing those 88 keys have taught me to have patience and endurance when learning challenging tasks."

- - **Explanation:** The writer of the excerpt above has established ethos by explaining his involvement with playing the piano for a long period of time. His expertise on piano playing can more likely cause readers to believe that he is an expert in the field of music. The scholarship readers may be more understanding of how his musical experiences relate to his academic goals.

- Pathos is an appeal to emotions. Your job as a writer is to persuade the reader by drawing on emotions such as sadness, joy, or anger. It is essential to use pathos when you are attempting to draw an emotional connection with your reader. Different ways to appeal to emotions are by telling short stories or using details that describe the emotions of the subject or person.

  - **Example of Pathos:** "When I first started high school, I did not have the best grades. I misbehaved in my classes and did not listen to my teachers. Although they thought I was a bad student, the real reason for my misbehavior was due to my parents' divorce. As a result, my grades slipped. I had a 2.0 G.P.A. But, I had one teacher who motivated me that I could do better. She told me that I was the captain of my own ship. With those words of motivation, I applied to college. Yes, I may have been silly to apply, but I needed to make a change. After waiting anxiously for months, one day I opened an admissions letter to my top college of choice! I was so glad, and knew that this next step would be the start to my journey of success."

- **Explanation:** In the above excerpt, the writer uses the pathos appeal by guiding the reader through the journey of his downfalls to his goal of success. The writer tells a story of how he was not the model student in high school due to his low grade point average. Many readers may sympathize with the writer because divorce is often challenging for young people to handle. As the writer continues to tell his story using details to describe his emotions, such as "waiting anxiously," the reader moves through the journey alongside the writer. It is the hope of the writer for an emotional connection to be established by his telling of his journey from trials to triumph.

In addition to the use of those three rhetorical appeals, you can also compare topics to everyday situations or people such as celebrities, athletes, or television characters. Analogies are also a way to set yourself apart from other applicants. For example, you may want to compare yourself to a cheetah. You may be fast, swift, and eager to pursue your visions and dreams. Overall, setting yourself apart provides the reader of your scholarship essay a unique experience and can cause your essay to be memorable.

## Your Turn to Write!

What or who can you compare yourself to? Do you have similar characteristics like a certain animal? Do you have similar characteristics as a famous athlete or leader of the past? Write about a comparison you share below.

# 6. WRITING THE CONCLUSION

The conclusion of the essay summarizes the main topics you presented for your reader. It serves as a closing statement to the points you presented in your scholarship essay. In your conclusion, include the main topic of your essay, along with a summary of the main points. Often times, it is advised to leave a lasting impression on the reader by addressing the larger purpose or goal of your essay. For example, if you are writing about how you will use scholarship funds for college, you could end your essay by showing how being able to purchase supplies will enable you to have a fulfilling, academic experience with less worry about financial costs. You could state how a fulfilling, academic experience can help you to reach your career goals. After writing your conclusion, re-read your scholarship essay to check if your conclusion provides a supportive, closing statement for your thoughts.

## 7. REVISING AND EDITING

After drafting the scholarship essay, two review processes are essential to perform. Those two processes are revising and editing.

**Revising** focuses on the larger order concerns of the paper such as organization, content, and a close look at the argument presented. Below is a checklist of questions to answer when revising your scholarship essay.

### **Revision Checklist**

- ☐ Does the essay address the prompt? Are all the key words addressed from the prompt?

*Introduction*
- ☐ Is the introduction creative?
- ☐ Does the introduction include a few general sentences about the topic?
- ☐ Does the introduction end with a thesis statement?
- ☐ Does the thesis statement state the main point of the scholarship essay?

*Body Paragraphs*
- Are the body paragraphs ordered logically? For example, do the events discussed follow the same order in which they occurred?
- Should some paragraphs be placed in a different order?
- Do each of the body paragraphs have a topic sentence?
- Are you referring to the topics presented in the prompt?
- Did you provide transitions between ideas, sentences, and paragraphs?

*Conclusion*
- Did you restate the main points from your essay in summary form?
- Did you restate your thesis statement? Do not merely repeat the same exact sentence; restructure the sentence.
- Did you show the larger purpose or goal of the scholarship essay? Do you answer a "so what?"
- Did you think your conclusion will leave a lasting impression on your reader?

*Creativity*
- Did you use at least one of the three rhetorical appeals: ethos, logos, or pathos?

- Do you attempt to set yourself apart by discussing your favorite experiences or writing your essay in a way that is compelling, detailed, and has descriptive language?
- Are there some sentences or words that can be removed? These sentences or words may not be relevant to the essay, or you may need to delete them to stay within the word count.

**Editing** focuses on lower order concerns such as grammar, word choice, and sentence structure.

Below is a checklist of questions to answer when revising your scholarship essay.

### **Editing Checklist**

- Are all your sentences full sentences and not fragments?
  - Sentences contain a full thought with at least one noun and a verb.
    - Example:
      *Sentence:* My mother is my hero because she inspires me to be a great student.
      *Fragment:* Then, once I knew that.

- Do you avoid run-on sentences and comma splices?
  - Run-on sentences have two independent clauses, while comma slices are an incorrect way to join independent clauses. Read through your essay and

be sure that all independent clauses are completed with the correct punctuation as explained below.

## Run-On Sentences:

Example:

*Run-On Sentence:* Scholarship funds will be useful to me as a future college student because I can purchase a new laptop for my classes the laptop will enable me to do my homework in my dorm room.

*One Version of a Corrected Sentence*: Scholarship funds will be useful to me as a future college student because I can purchase a new laptop for my classes. **(independent clause)** The laptop will enable me to do my homework in my dorm room. **(independent clause)**

Ways to correct a run-on sentence are using a semicolon between two independent clauses, a period to separate the two clauses, or a comma with a coordinating conjunction or FANBOYS such as "for," "and," "nor," "but," "or," "yet," or "so." In the above sentence, I used a period to separate the independent clauses.

**Comma Splice:**

Example:

*Comma Splice*: Scholarship funds will be useful to me as a future college student because I can purchase a new laptop for my classes, the laptop will enable me to do my homework in my dorm room.

The sentence above contains a comma splice because the writer inserted a comma between two independent clauses. A comma cannot join independent clauses alone, so ways to fix a comma splice are by using the same rules to correct a run-on sentence.

- Is there variety of sentence structure? Are some sentences long while others are shorter to add variation of lengths to your essay? Are some sentences simple, compound, complex, or compound-complex?

Examples:
*Simple Sentence:* I love to learn about space.

*Compound Sentence:* I love to learn about space, so I plan to major in astrology.

*Complex Sentence:* Although I have other interests such as cooking, I want to learn more about constellations.

*Compound-Complex Sentence*: Since *Hidden Figures* is my favorite movie, I want to become a world-changer by using my knowledge about space, just like the pioneers in the movie.

- Is the vocabulary clear and effective? Do not merely use words to sound fancy! Sometimes a "simple" word can be more effective to your reader than a "fancy" word. Try to be as familiar with your words as possible. Read through your essay and search for words that can be substituted for others. Avoid jargon that may only be understood by people in a certain community of people, such as medical or law terms. You never know who may be reading your essay. A thesaurus can help.

- Do you repeat the same words? Are you able to substitute some words to avoid redundancy or repetition?

- Do you use the correct words? Be careful not to confuse words such as "to, two, and too," "it's (it is) and "its," or "they're (they are), their, and there."

☐ Did you spell check your essay?

These are a few tips for revising and editing your scholarship essay. I will suggest that you read over your essay in multiple settings. Read it aloud, in front of a mirror, outdoors, or even read it from end to beginning. By reading the essay in these various ways, you may be able to catch mistakes that you missed while writing. Also, ask a friend, family member, teacher, or a trusted individual to read over your essay as well. Ask them if they were on the scholarship committee, would they award you the funds?

## 8. SAVING/RECYCLING THE ESSAY

Save your scholarship essay because losing your hard work would be devastating! I advise you to save your scholarship essay in multiple locations. Some places include on a personal computer, on a flash drive, or by sending it to your personal/school email account.

Also, save your essay in multiple locations because you never know when you may need it. For example, you may see a scholarship posting online while at school. If your essay is saved in your email, then you can retrieve it easier than if it was on a flash drive in your dorm.

In addition, keep a skeleton version of your essay because you may be able to use the essay again. A skeleton version of the essay is not as specific to a certain prompt, but it can be modified to fit a prompt specifically. Therefore, save all versions of your scholarship essays because you may be able to use them again.

## 9. PRACTICE WRITING THE SCHOLARSHIP ESSAY

# Your Turn to Write!

Practice can help you develop your skill for writing scholarship essays. The more you practice, the better you may become. I have included a standard scholarship essay prompt below. Using the steps we have discussed, draft a scholarship essay.

*"How will the scholarship funds assist you in reaching your goals?"*

Keywords/Ideas:
_____
_____
_____
_____
_____
_____

Introduction:
_____
_____
_____

Thesis:


Body Paragraph 1:

Body Paragraph 2:

Body Paragraph 3:

_____
_____
_____
_____
_____
_____
_____
_____
_____
_____
_____
_____
_____
_____
_____
_____

Conclusion:

_____
_____
_____
_____
_____

## 10. USES OF SCHOLARSHIP FUNDS

If awarded a scholarship, there are various ways to spend the funds. Scholarships range from as low as $10 to as much as $10,000. To avoid spending the money carelessly, below are a few ways to invest the scholarship funds in ways that can bring great return.

*1. Save*

When you receive your scholarship funds, no matter the amount, save some of the money. Students often times will purchase luxuries that were maybe once unattainable. Some students purchase cars, while others purchase designer clothing. But, why spend thousands of dollars on one or two purchases of material value? Advice: Save at least 40 % of scholarship award. You want to be financially secure during and after college. Therefore set money aside that you can use in case you are unable to receive a lump sum of funds in the future.

*2. Purchase Necessary Educational Supplies*

Scholarship funds can be used to purchase supplies, equipment, and books. Some of these items may include a laptop, hard drive, paper, pens, a printer, tablet or calculator. Also, one college textbook could cost $250, and you could spend up to $1,000 total on college textbooks per semester. So, use the scholarship funds to purchase any necessary educational supplies you may need.

3. *Travel*

Awarded funds can also be used to travel. You can make memories by taking a fun trip alone, with classmates, friends or loved ones. Traveling enables you to gain new experiences and often broaden your worldview. Students who travel are often more marketable to employers, academic admissions advisors, or internship committees because these persons sometimes view the students as well-rounded individuals who are open to trying new adventures.

4. *Give*

Poet Maya Angelou said, "When you learn, teach. When you get, give." Giving is truly a testament of appreciation for the funds you were granted through your scholarship, so give to those who may be less fortunate than you. A local shelter, classroom, or even a friend may be in need, and you have the power to contribute to their success as you have been granted.

5. *Cover Unexpected Costs*

Life happens. When it does, it is best to be financially prepared. You may suddenly need a new tire or money to visit the doctor after an unexpected illness. Some occurrences are unexpected, so it is good to save some of your scholarship money for a rainy day, family emergency, or an unexpected event.

## CONCLUSION

I hope you have enjoyed learning steps of writing a scholarship essay. Please take these tips and apply them to your writing. Continuously refer to more resources and pass the information along to your family members, friends, and classmates. Writing takes time, dedication, and focus, so be prepared to take the journey.

*"Start writing no matter what.*
*The water does not flow until the faucet is turned on."*
– Louis L'Amour

# SAMPLE WINNING SCHOLARSHIP ESSAY

**Regions Riding Forward Scholarship Winner**
**$2,500 prize**
**Written By: Candace Chambers, Age 19, College Freshman**

Prompt: "Who inspires you? Is there a particular African-American who inspires you because of the significant achievements in our society that he or she has been responsible for? In 500 words or less: Address how an African-American has been an inspiration in your life. Discuss the contributions of the African-American individual who has served to inspire and motivate you."

### "Fighting Fires of Injustice"

I am a firefighter. When fires arise, I bring the hose. 50 years ago, one of my fellow firefighters died fighting the fire of racial injustice, voter suppression, and inequality. Medgar Evers, Mississippi's first field secretary for the NAACP during times of unfair exclusions and persecutions demonstrated perseverance and courageous spirit by pressing toward the mark of equal voting rights. In a state of sweltering injustice, Evers organized voter registrations and spent many hours working to ensure that African Americans had an equal opportunity to cast a ballot, even though contrary to the standard way of life in the state he called home.

Firefighter Evers has been an inspiration to me in my pursuit of my dreams. His urge for change has motivated me to educate the minds of young individuals. For example, I notice how injustices are evident in the public school systems, with some students possessing the latest technological equipment such as promethium boards in their classrooms, while others, whose schools are located in underprivileged areas are still dusting chalk off of their clothes. I notice how some students of color are educated to "pass" and not educated to live in a world full of opportunities. Fairness is essential in educating the future, and I want to be an advocate for change.

As a leader, Evers took the initiative to put out the fires that were damaging the unity of Mississippi. With my major of English Education, I will bring water to extinguish the setbacks affecting my students and broaden their scope of life through literature and analyzing the language. Through teaching, I will compare how in the novel, *To Kill a Mockingbird*, Atticus Finch has a strong willed stance against injustice, just as Medgar Evers refused to deter his decision to apply to the University of Mississippi's Law School in 1964, despite opposition from the campus. My students will become aware of how Evers investigated the killing of Emmitt Till, a 14-year-old boy who was murdered after allegedly gesturing to a White woman, and how they too can stop the violence in their communities to save another life from the wounds of a bullet.

As the alarm buzzes loudly in the fire station, firefighters prepare to conquer blazing, scorching flames by gearing up their mind, body, and spirit. They know that the fire may be their last to tackle, but the challenge is at hand and the goal must be met. Not only are firefighters dressed in suits of armor designed for the pressure of heat, but everyday heroes take on obstacles to meet destined ambitions.

Evers fought his last fire on the night of June 12, 1963 after he was shot on the porch of his home in Jackson, Mississippi surrounded by the cries of his wife and three small children.

Firefighter Evers' life will not be in vain. Firefighter Chambers is ready to drench the ills of society by educating one child at a time.

## Analysis of "Fighting Fires of Injustice"

[An analogy is used to open the essay to compare the writer to a firefighter.]

I am a firefighter. When fires arise, I bring the hose. 50 years ago, one of my fellow firefighters died fighting the fire of racial injustice, voter suppression, and inequality. Medgar Evers, Mississippi's first field secretary for the NAACP during times of unfair exclusions and persecutions demonstrated perseverance and courageous spirit by pressing toward the mark of equal voting rights. In a state of sweltering injustice, Evers organized voter registrations and spent many hours working to ensure that African Americans had an equal opportunity to cast a ballot, even though contrary to the standard way of life in the state he called home. [Clear, concise thesis statement]

[Topic Sentence] Firefighter Evers has been an inspiration to me in my pursuit of my dreams. His urge for change has motivated me to educate the minds of young individuals. For example, I notice how injustices are evident in the public school systems, with some students possessing the latest technological equipment such as promethium boards in their classrooms, while others, whose schools are located in underprivileged areas are still dusting chalk off of their clothes. I notice how some students of color are educated to "pass" and not educated to live in a world full of opportunities. Fairness is essential in educating the future, and I want to be an advocate for change.

[Transition] As a leader, Evers took the initiative to put out the fires that were damaging the unity of Mississippi. With my major of English Education, I will bring water to extinguish the setbacks affecting my students and broaden their scope of life through literature and analyzing the language. Through teaching, I will compare how in the novel, *To Kill a Mockingbird*, Atticus Finch has a strong willed stance against injustice, just as Medgar Evers refused to deter his decision to apply to the University of Mississippi's Law School in 1964, despite opposition from the campus. My students will become aware of how Evers investigated the killing of Emmitt Till, a 14-year-old boy who was murdered after allegedly gesturing to a White woman, and how they too can stop the violence in their communities to save another life from the wounds of a bullet.

As the alarm buzzes loudly in the fire station, firefighters prepare to conquer blazing, scorching flames by gearing up their mind, body, and spirit. They know that the fire may be their last to tackle, but the challenge is at hand and the goal must be met. Not only are firefighters dressed in suits of armor designed for the pressure of heat, but everyday heroes take on obstacles to meet destined ambitions.

Evers fought his last fire on the night of June 12, 1963 after he was shot on the porch of his home in Jackson, Mississippi surrounded by the <u>cries of his wife and three small children.</u> [Sensory Details]

<u>Firefighter Evers' life will not be in vain. Firefighter Chambers is ready to drench the ills of society by educating one child at a time.</u>

[Conclusion restates Evers' role in fighting injustice while providing a call to action.]

## Resources

**Transitional Devices:**

- First
- Second
- Third
- Last
- Next
- Besides
- Finally
- Furthermore
- In addition
- However
- In comparison
- Sometimes
- Nevertheless
- Therefore
- For example
- In summary
- As a result

## Thinking Maps:

Bubble Map:

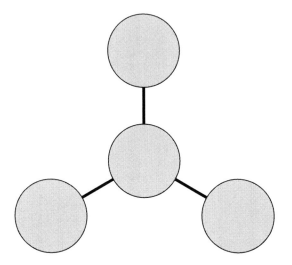

Venn Diagram:

## WORKS CITED

Bergen G, Stevens MR, Burns ER. Falls and Fall Injuries Among Adults Aged ≥65 Years — United States, 2014. MMWR Morb Mortal Wkly Rep 2016;65:993–998. DOI: http://dx.doi.org/10.15585/mmwr.mm6537a2.

Bureau of Labor Statistics, U.S. Department of Labor, *The Economics Daily*, College tuition and fees increase 63 percent since January 2006 on the Internet at https://www.bls.gov/opub/ted/2016/college-tuition-and-fees-increase-63-percent-since-january-2006.htm

"Healthy Schools." *Centers for Disease Control and Prevention*, Centers for Disease Control and Prevention, 16 May 2017, www.cdc.gov/healthyschools/nutrition/facts.htm.

"Hero." *Merriam-Webster*, Merriam-Webster, www.merriam webster.com/dictionary/hero.

"How Aid Is Calculated." *Federal Student Aid*, 1 Nov. 2017, studentaid.ed.gov/sa/fafsa/next-steps/how-calculated.

*State Financial Aid Programs*, www.nasfaa.org/State_Financial_Aid_Programs.

"Success Isn't about How Much Money You Make, It's about the Difference You Make in People's Lives. ~ Michelle Obama ( Inspirational Quotes ) | Daily Inspirational Quotes." *Daily Inspirational Quotes*, 1 Mar. 2016, www.dailyinspirationalquotes.in/2013/07/success-isnt-about-how-much-money-you-make-its-about-the-difference-you-make-in-peoples-lives-michelle-obama-inspirational-quotes/.

## ABOUT THE AUTHOR

Candace Chambers is an academic coach, writer, educator, and CEO of Educational Writing Services LLC. She has snagged over $80,000 in scholarships, grants, and assistantships over the course of her educational journey.

Candace is a scholar of English. She obtained her Bachelors of Arts in English with a concentration in education from Jackson State University in Jackson, Mississippi. She is a licensed educator for English, grades 7-12. In addition, she obtained her Masters of Arts degree with a concentration in Composition, Rhetoric, and English Studies from the University of Alabama. She has presented her research across the nation.

Candace has served in various capacities within the writing field. Her roles have included writing consultant at Jackson State University, University of Alabama, and Shelton State Community College. She was the instructor of record of freshman college composition courses at the University of Alabama, and also served as an Assistant Director of the campus writing center. While at Shelton State Community College, she served as writing consultant test prep leader for Accuplacer testing.

Candace is the recipient of various awards including the President's Future Leader scholarship award from the International Writing Center Association, Scholar for the Dream award from the Conference on College, Composition, and Communication, and was designated as a 2015 HBCU All-Star by the White House Initiative on Historically Black Colleges and Universities.

Made in the USA
Middletown, DE
16 October 2018